SPACE SONGS

FOR

CHILDREN

Fun Songs and Activities About Outer Space

SPACE SONGS

FOR

CHILDREN

Fun Songs and Activities About Outer Space

by Tonja Evetts Weimer

Pearce-Evetts Publishing

Pittsburgh, Pennsylvania

This book and audio cassette contain songs and activities about space, for children ages three to eight. The book is designed primarily for parents and teachers. It contains activities and additional resources to help make space even more exciting for the children.

Space Songs for Children

Fun Songs and Activities About Outer Space

By Tonja Evetts Weimer

Published by:

Pearce Evetts Publishing
P.O. Box 79117
Pittsburgh, PA 15216, U.S.A.
(412) 344-5451

© 1993 by Tonja Evetts Weimer.
All rights reserved.
Printed in the United States of America.
ISBN: 0-936823-11-9

Publisher's Cataloging in Publication
(Prepared by Quality Books Inc.)

Weimer, Tonja Evetts.
    Space songs for children: fun songs and activities about outer space/Tonja Evetts Weimer.
    p. cm.
    Includes bibliographical references.
    Preassigned LCCN: 93-85471.
    ISBN 0-936823-11-9

    1. Children's songs. 2. Outer space—Songs and music—Juvenile literature. 3. Outer space—Juvenile literature. I. Title.
M1997.W45 1993   782.42'159'083
                         QBI93-1133

CONTENTS

Author's Note	7
Acknowledgments	9
Introduction	11

Space Songs and Activities

1.	I Wish I Was	14
2.	Floatin' In The Bathtub	20
3.	Flies In The Cabin	26
4.	Five In The Bag	34
5.	In My Rocket	38
6.	Cloud Lullaby	42
7.	Get On Board	48
8.	The Milky Way	52
9.	I Love My Moon	56
10.	Riding In My Space Buggy	62
11.	Jumping To Jupiter	68
12.	Little Windows	74

Bibliography and Resources

Glossary of Space Terms - Definitions for Children	83
Supplemental Materials	85
Annotated Bibliography on Children's Books Relating to Aviation and Space	86
Resource Centers	98
About the Author	101
Other Materials from Tonja Evetts Weimer	103

AUTHOR'S NOTE

In 1992, I gave a presentation, "Fingerplays and Action Songs," at the National Association for the Education of Young Children Annual Conference in New Orleans. Fortunately, Dr. Jane Hodges, Aerospace Education Specialist from NASA (National Aeronautics and Space Administration) was in the audience. After the presentation, she suggested I expand into the aerospace world, as there was very little available in the field. I spent a few days thinking about the type of songs I might write and put a few of them together. When I sang them to Dr. Hodges and a few other friends, the response was so positive, I decided to explore the idea a little more.

A few weeks later, my husband and I flew down to see the launch of space orbiter Discovery. I spent time in the space museums, becoming more familiar with terms, vocabulary, projects, and equipment. I visited NASA offices and talked with some of the people who work in the space program. I visited a "space" daycare center and sang some of my newly written space songs with the children there. The children danced and acted the songs out with total abandon. Whatever reservations I might have had were almost dissolved. I was rapidly coming down with "Space Fever."

The day of the launch arrived, and it seemed that we had to get up in the middle of the night. We boarded a V.I.P. bus and rode to the launch site. The launch was delayed a few hours due to overcast conditions. Finally, the sun came out. It was actually going to happen. We stood at Banana Creek, in front of the set of bleachers where many people sat, counting down with the clock and the other observers. 5, 4, 3, 2, 1, BLAST OFF!

I was unprepared. I had no idea how beautiful this event would be. The sky thundered, the ground beneath our feet shook, and this enormous rocket rose in front of us, filling the atmosphere with noise and color and cloud. I stood there, filled with reverence, and full of emotion. I was completely caught off guard.

I could not find words to express what I was thinking or feeling for the next days and weeks. But songs were pouring out of me. I could not stop them. I wrote one on the way home on the plane, another one in the shower the next morning. And on and on it went, until I had 12 complete songs.

One cannot be around NASA for long without absorbing some of the enthusiasm for the space program. I hope the music presented here helps you catch the "fever" too.

Tonja Evetts Weimer
March 23, 1993
Pittsburgh, Pennsylvania

ACKNOWLEDGMENTS

I thank Dr. Jane Hodges for introducing the space experience to me. To feel so inspired, and to have a channel for that creative flow is rich. I was lucky to have the opportunity to attend a launch, and I was lucky to have a way to put that experience into form.

I also want to thank the other people at NASA who gave me inspiration through their talent, dedication and heart. Thanks to Astronaut Jim Voss, for being gracious and supportive of my aerospace music. Thanks to Astronaut Fred Gregory for supporting Early Childhood Space Education programs, and taking a genuine interest in them. Thanks to the other astronauts, engineers, and support staff who make our space program the triumph that it is.

Thanks also to Vaughn Lofstead for his music and guidance through this album; to Manuela Bernardez for art work; to Ed Lafferty for his careful and caring editing; to Linda Ho for her typesetting; to Dr. Norman Sanger for his copyright research; to Cindy Nail and Billie Phillips for listening and encouraging when the songs were brand new, and to Colleen and Jim Datillo for the same. Special thanks to Miss Julia Datillo for her artistic ideas for book jacket design.

There were many other people who encouraged and cheered as I wrote song after song, and called them on the telephone to sing to them. Lois Durant, Judy Lawrence Basta, Karlene Bennett, Dr. Roberta Ralston Dimond, and Julie Stauffer Carville all listened with love and insight. Further encouragement came from Ellie Galbraith, Linda Hardie, Mary Meyer, Dr. Saundra DiPento, Christine Simmons, Dr. Janene Varner, Nancy and Anthony Lardo, Joan Fernsler and my support staff, Kathy Duggan and Therese Brown. Special acknowledgment goes to Linda Ard, for sharing her article, "A Resource Unit for the Moon," Texas Child Care Quarterly, Fall 1988. And a big thanks to Miss Melissa Brown, four years old, for her enthusiastic dancing to every song I sang, as I practiced for the taping sessions.

Lastly, I thank my family. To Vik Pearce, my husband, for the hard work he puts into these projects, and for supporting all of my efforts. To my children, Malini, Aneysha, Kenny and Alli, for listening to their mom's songs over and over and never acting bored. And to my parents, Hoke and Alma Evetts, for teaching me to always do my best, and that is the best there is.

INTRODUCTION

Outer space is a topic that fascinates young children. It addresses the child's innate sense of wonder at the universe. Studying outer space also promotes a better understanding of our own planet.

At a very early age, children begin to ask such questions as, "Where do the clouds go? How high is up? What are stars? Why does the moon shine?", and hundreds of other why questions about the world, the sky, and what they can see for themselves. They also have some awareness of the space program, rockets and astronauts from television and other media presentations. It seems only fitting, therefore, that we have songs and activities that can address their natural curiosity, and build their information base.

Concepts of time, distance, and space are abstractions that can be difficult however, for young children to grasp. A long time to young children is their next birthday. A great distance is five hours in a car or a plane to Grandma's house. The amount of space or distance they travel is not real to them; the time it takes to get there is how they measure it. The parent or teacher must find some tangible activities about this subject matter that the child can become engaged in, to make the information more relevant and age-appropriate.

The songs on this tape and the activities in this book were written from the child's perspective. How would it feel to be on the moon, and a long way from home? What would "no gravity" mean to me or my Mom or Dad? What would dinner-time in a space ship be like, if my food could float?

I hope the songs and activities will address some of the thoughts and feelings for the child, and open up new vistas of ideas to be considered. Most of all, I hope the songs contribute something that makes the space experience more personal and meaningful to the child and to the adults they are sharing it with.

So... let's head on out to the Milky Way. I'll meet you there.

SPACE SONGS

AND

ACTIVITIES

1.

I WISH I WAS

*Traditional folk tune; words
by Tonja Evetts Weimer*

This song is about objects in the sky that children can see. Make up your own motions to go with each verse. Acting a song out helps children remember it better.

SPACE SONGS FOR CHILDREN

Key of C: Chords C, F and G7

```
  C            F           C
I wish I was the sun up in the sky,

  C                          G7
I wish I was the sun up in the sky,

    C
If I was the sun up in the sky,

      F
I'd shine on you when you passed by,

    C          F     G7    C
I wish I was the sun up in the sky.

  C          F    G7    C
I wish I was a winkin' blinkin' star,

  C                         G7
I wish I was a winkin' blinkin' star,

    C
If I was a winkin' blinkin' star,

      F
I'd wink at you wherever you are,

    C          F    G7    C
I wish I was a winkin' blinkin' star.
```

```
C               F    G7   C
```
I wish I was the moon over-head,

```
C                          G7
```
I wish I was the moon over-head,

```
   C
```
If I was the moon overhead

```
    F
```
I'd shine on you when you were in bed,

```
   C           F    G7   C
```
I wish I was the moon over-head.

Activities or Song Extenders:

This song is a good introduction to the solar system.

- Show pictures, posters, mobiles, slides and videos of the solar system. Name and identify the sun, moon, and stars, and move on to naming the planets. The children will have more activities about planets in the song, "Jumping To Jupiter."

- Have children do art projects related to the solar system. Cut the shapes of the moon (full, quarter, and crescent), stars and sun, out of thin sponge. Children can dip them in paint and then touch them onto paper to make prints or to make designs. Have the children make a mural of "Things I can see in the sky." Label their drawings, and encourage their discussion of what they can see.

- Discuss the size of the planets in relation to each other. Design a mobile out of styrofoam balls to make the concept of our solar system more real.

- Explain that everything we see in outer space is very far away (the sun, moon and stars). Some stars are as big or bigger than the sun, but they look small because they are so distant. Take children outside, and have several children walk away. Point out to the children how much smaller they seem the farther away they get. Observe cars going down the street or road. Notice how big they are when they are close, and how small they look as they drive farther away. At what point can you not see them anymore? Make these observations daily when you are on walks with the children, until they become familiar with the concept. Then, when you discuss "far-away," they will have some personal experience as a reference.

- Explain that if you could drive by car on a highway, it would take five months without stopping to get to the moon, and 190 years to get to the sun.

- This could be a good time to introduce binoculars, and eventually a telescope, to show how things can be brought closer. Take a trip to a planetarium to see telescopes of a large size.

2.

FLOATIN' IN THE BATHTUB

*Words and music
by Tonja Evetts Weimer*

Astronauts are very talented, intelligent, educated, dedicated people who have to go through rigorous training before they can go into space. Part of their training is to be submerged in tanks of water, wearing their airtight space suits, while they simulate working on spacecraft and space modules. This underwater experience is preparation for what they will be doing out in space in an environment of weightlessness. Floating in water is one of the few ways we have here on Earth to duplicate the weightless experience in space.

Key of G: Chords G, C, and D7

Chorus

> G
> Floatin' in the bathtub, swimmin' in the pool,
>
> C
> I'm gettin' ready, for astronaut school,
>
> G
> Floatin' in the bathtub, swimmin' in the pool,
>
> C   D7   G
> I'll be an astronaut, 'cause I am so cool.

Verse

> G   C   G
> My mama says her diet's no good,
>
> G   C   D7
> She wants to go to space with me,
>
> G   C   G
> She thinks she can eat all she wants,
>
>   C   D7
> And float around weightless-ly,

Chorus

> D7   G
> Oh, I'm floatin' in the ...

FLOATIN' IN THE BATHTUB

Verse

```
    G              C   G
My Daddy hates to exer-cise,

    G          C        D7
Push-ups just make him wheeze,

     G              C       G
But if he came out in space with me,

        C         D7
He'd look like HERCU-LES!
```

Chorus

```
    D7      G
Oh, I'm floatin' in the ...
```

Verse

```
    G                C    G
I'm going to take my dog into space,

    G              C    D7
He'll like it 'cause there are no fleas,

       G              C   G
But when he gets out, to run around,

        C             D7
He's gonna miss all those trees...
```

Chorus

```
    D7      G
Oh, I'm floatin' in the...
```

Verse

```
    G                    C          G
I'm taking some of my toys with me,

    G       C          D7
I'll play all night and all day,

     G                 C          G
But when my mom says clean them up,

          C                    D7
She'll just see them floatin' a-way,
```

Chorus

```
    D7       G
Oh, I'm floatin' in the ...
```

Activities or Song Extenders:

- Discuss with children how it feels to swim in the pool or float in the bathtub, and how that is related to the feeling of weightlessness.

- Discuss how gravity keeps us from falling off of the Earth. Explain how spaceships, missiles and rockets have to go very fast and high to get away from the Earth's gravity.

  Activities to explore gravity are:

1. Jump from a block or a box. Ask children, "Why do you go down?" Explore jumping from different levels and heights, supervised, and continue to explain why one goes down, instead of up when they jump. Ask children how high they can jump. Why can't they jump higher? (The Earth's gravity pulls them down.) Discuss what it would feel like to jump on the moon. (The moon has some gravity. If a person weighs 60 pounds on Earth, they would weigh about 10 pounds on the moon. Hence, they would be very light and be able to jump very high.)

2. Drop different objects from different levels, such as from the jungle gym, the slide, a chair, a ladder. Do any go up? Do some fall faster than others? Why?

3. Ask children to hold their arms up and out. Ask them how long they can hold them there. Are they getting tired? Why? (Gravity is pulling them down.)

- Create a new dance to this song called the "Space Swim". Let children make up their own "swimming" dance as you sing and play this song. Do the dance again when they have their pretend space suits on. If you can, take pictures or video of the children when they are doing this.

- Create a "band" to play along with this song. Use some old guitars for children to dramatize with. Also use other rhythm instruments. Give the band a name, such as, "Space-Man Band," or "The Moon Rockers." Introduce the use of a microphone. Use a real one or a pretend one.

3.

FLIES IN THE CABIN

*Tune: Skip To My Lou;
words and adaptation
by Tonja Evetts Weimer*

Simple habits we take for granted in living on Earth are altered dramatically when there is a lack of gravity. This song introduces what it would be like to eat meals in a spaceship. Some of the consequences could be quite amusing.

SPACE SONGS FOR CHILDREN

Key of C: Chords C, F, and G7

Verse

C
Flies in the cabin, shoo fly, shoo,

G7
Flies in the cabin, shoo fly, shoo,

C
Flies in the cabin, shoo fly, shoo,

F   G7   C
Shoo to my Lou my darling.

Chorus

C
Shoo, shoo, shoo to my Lou,

G7
Shoo, shoo, shoo to my Lou,

C
Shoo, shoo, shoo to my Lou,

F   G7   C
Shoo to my Lou my darling.

FLIES IN THE CABIN

Verse

C
Dinner in a space ship is gooey goo goo,

G7
Dinner in a space ship is gooey goo goo,

C
Dinner in a space ship is gooey goo goo,

F   G7   C
Sing to my Lou my darling.

Chorus

C
Sing, sing, sing to my Lou etc. (substitute sing for shoo)

Verse

C
I dropped my meatball, what'll I do?

G7
I dropped my meatball, what'll I do?

C
I dropped my meatball, what'll I do?

```
F        G7      C
```
Roll to my Lou my darling.

Chorus

```
C
```
Roll, roll, roll to my Lou, etc.

Verse

```
C
```
It's floating off, over towards you,

```
G7
```
It's floating off, over towards you,

```
C
```
It's floating off, over towards you,

```
F        G7      C
```
Float to my Lou my darling.

Chorus

```
C
```
Float, float, float to my Lou, etc.

Verse

```
C
```
Open your mouth and chew, chew, chew,

G7
Open your mouth and chew, chew, chew,

C
Open your mouth and chew, chew, chew,

F   G7   C
Chew to my Lou my darling.

Chorus

C
Chew, chew, chew to my Lou, etc.

Activities or Song Extenders:

- Children love to act this song out as they sing it. Let them take turns singing and dramatizing the words. Use some musical instruments, such as rhythm sticks, tone blocks, bells, triangles or drums to accentuate the beat, or for the different verses.

- The evolution of what astronauts used to eat (they squeezed very unappetizing food out of a tube) and what they can eat now can be discussed. Today's astronauts have over a hundred different food items such as cereals, spaghetti, scrambled eggs, and twenty varieties of drinks to choose from. There is no refrigerator on board, so many foods have been dehydrated (had the water removed). Water is then added at meal time and the food is heated in an oven. Cans, flexible pouches, and plastic containers are used for packaging. Because of limited space, there are weight and storage restrictions. Astronauts eat three balanced meals a day of about three thousand calories. This gives them their needed supply of potassium, calcium and nitrogen, which the body loses in weightlessness. Loss of these minerals affects muscle tone, bone mass, ability to concentrate and disposition.

- Foods that can be eaten in space can be prepared with the children. Natural foods (with no water removed) are also taken on the shuttle. Take some of the following items with you when you dramatize riding in your spaceship: apples, raisins, peanuts, graham crackers, fruit drinks, and instant chocolate milk. Use this opportunity to discuss eating balanced meals (as the astronauts do!) with the children, and how if they don't, they may become tired or cranky. Practice eating your food slowly and carefully (also as the astronauts do!), so it won't float away.

- Here is a list of more foods eaten in space:
  applesauce
  bananas
  beef stroganoff with noodles
  bread
  apple drink
  orange drink
  cereal
  chicken and rice
  cookies
  eggs
  food bars
  shrimp
  cocoa
  green beans
  nuts
  puddings
  spaghetti and sauce
  tuna
  grape drink

4.

FIVE IN THE BAG

*Traditional folk tune; words
by Tonja Evetts Weimer*

This song is fun to dramatize. It introduces how astronauts sleep in space and what happens with a lack of gravity.

Key of C : Chords C, F, and G7

    C
There were 5 in the bag,

    C
And the little one nagged,

    C   F C   F C
Roll o-ver, Roll o-ver,

          F   G7   C
So they all rolled over and one floated off!

Repeat with numbers counting backwards.

(Last verse)

    C
There were none in the bag,

    C
And the little one nagged,

    F   C   G7   C
Come back! Get in the sack!

Activities or Song Extenders:

- Discuss the different ways astronauts can sleep in space (upright, lying down, sitting in a chair), and why they would need to be fastened to something (there is no gravity, so they would float around the cabin). Astronauts sleep in sleeping bags, which keeps them in one place when they are sleeping. If their arms are out of the bag, however, they "float" out in front of them.

- Discuss why the astronauts might need to wear sleeping masks. (It is daylight every forty-five minutes, as they orbit the Earth.)

- This song is an opportunity for very young children to practice their counting. Be sure to do the fingerplay motions when you sing it.

- There are other songs that will reinforce these concepts, as you proceed through the songs and activities.

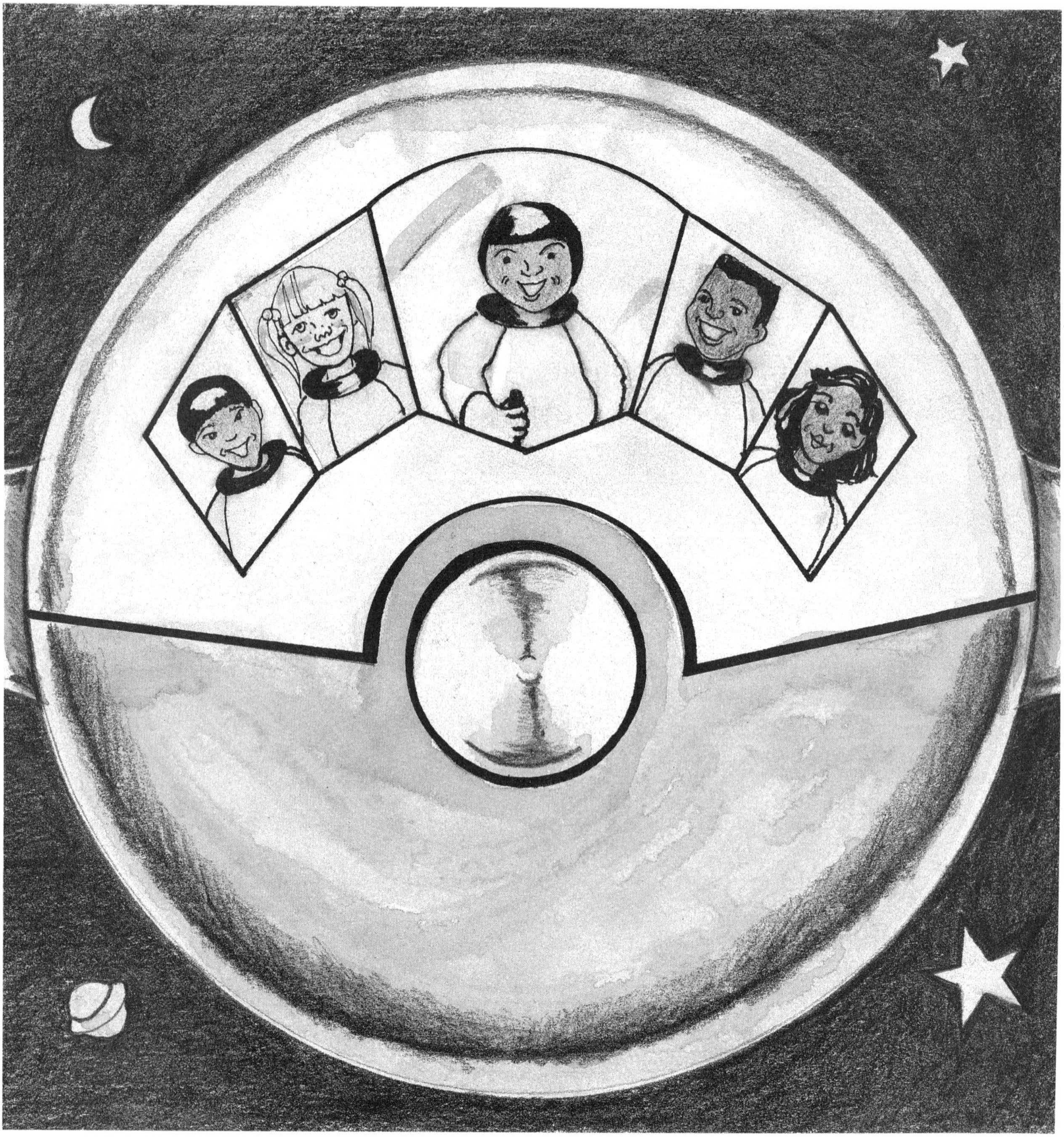

5.

IN MY ROCKET

*Traditional tune;
words and adaptation
by Tonja Evetts Weimer*

This song introduces the concept of the countdown before lift-off, and teaches young children to count backwards. It also presents the astronaut as a "hero" model to young children. This is a significant contribution to children's lives, since they need role models to imitate. Astronauts are men and women from many ethnic backgrounds, with superlative qualifications and dedication to their jobs.

SPACE SONGS FOR CHILDREN

Key of C: Chords C, F, and G7

10, 9, 8, 7, 6, 5, 4, 3, 2, 1 ... BLAST OFF!

Verse

```
C            F     G7
In my rocket see me ride,

G7              C
With my crew by my side,

C                F
Watching planets, all day long,

G7               C
I'm an astronaut, brave and strong.
```

Chorus

```
C                       F       G7
Flying up, flying up, high and away,

G7                   C
Flying up through the sky and away,

C                F
Watching planets all day long,

G7                 C
I'm an astronaut, brave and strong.
```

Verse

```
C              F    G7
In my shuttle, see me glide,
```

```
G7              C
```
With my crew by my side,

```
C             F
```
Watching Earth, all day long,

```
G7              C
```
I'm an astronaut, brave and strong.

Repeat chorus.

Substitute "Earth" for "planets" in second chorus.

Activities and Song Extenders:

- To stimulate dramatic play, provide round and cone-shaped blocks if children want to build rocket ships. Large cardboard boxes (that refrigerators or other appliances were packaged in) can also be shaped and painted into the shapes of spaceships.

- Have dress-up clothes of helmets, boots, gloves, and zip-on jump suits for children to dramatize being an astronaut.

- Display authentic space pictures on the walls of the areas where children are building their rockets or gliders. Also display pictures of some of the astronauts, and learn some of their names. For children five and older, learn the names of some of the missions the astronauts flew on. (See Resources)

- The concept of the shuttle as a glider can also be introduced in this song. Make a glider and discuss what makes it fly, or purchase small easy-to-make glider planes made of balsa wood, or paper. (Once you have the model for a glider, you can construct one yourself from the styrofoam meat or vegetable trays you get in the supermarket.)

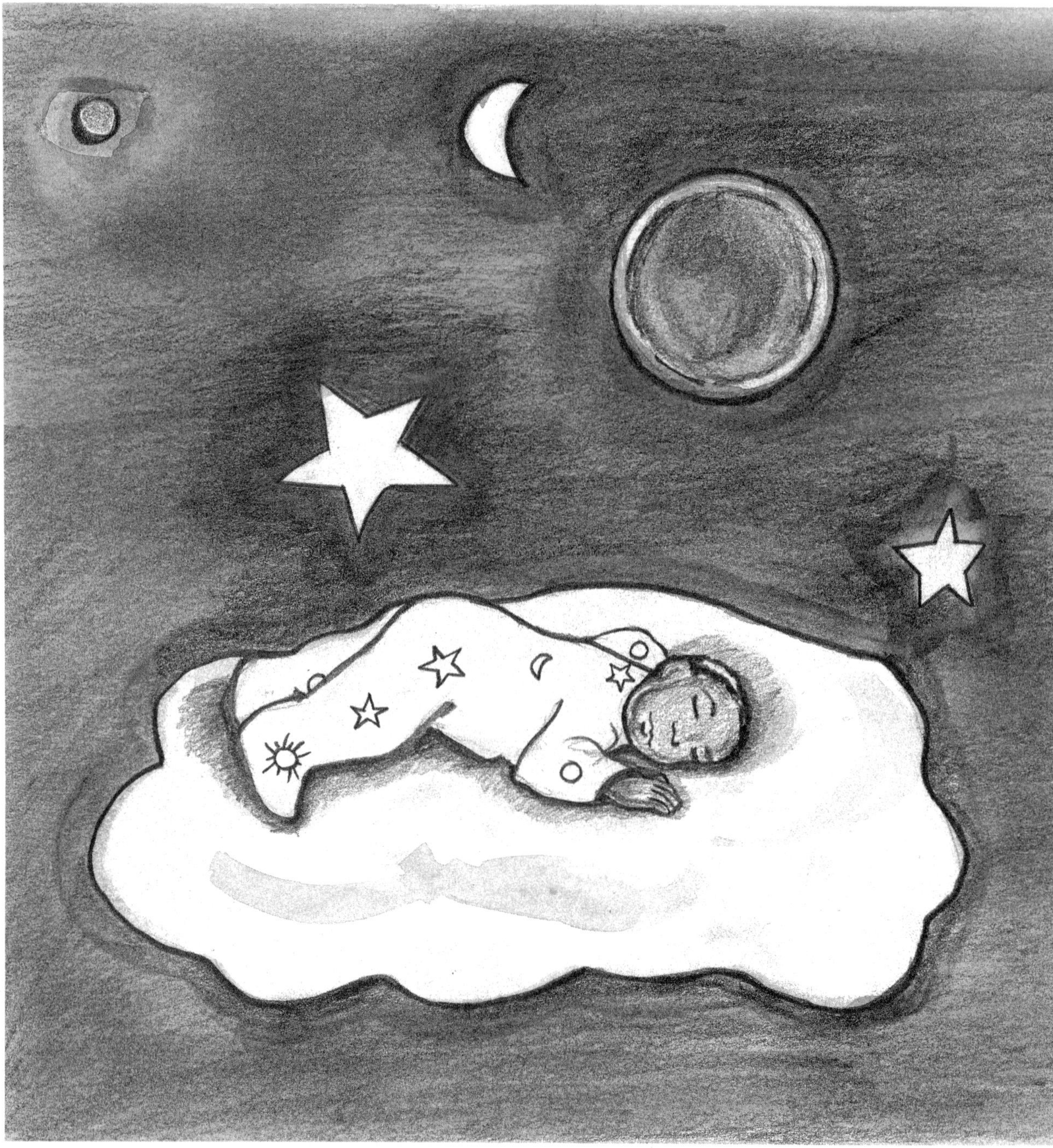

6.

CLOUD LULLABY

Words and music by Tonja Evetts Weimer

This is a rest song for nap time or bed time.

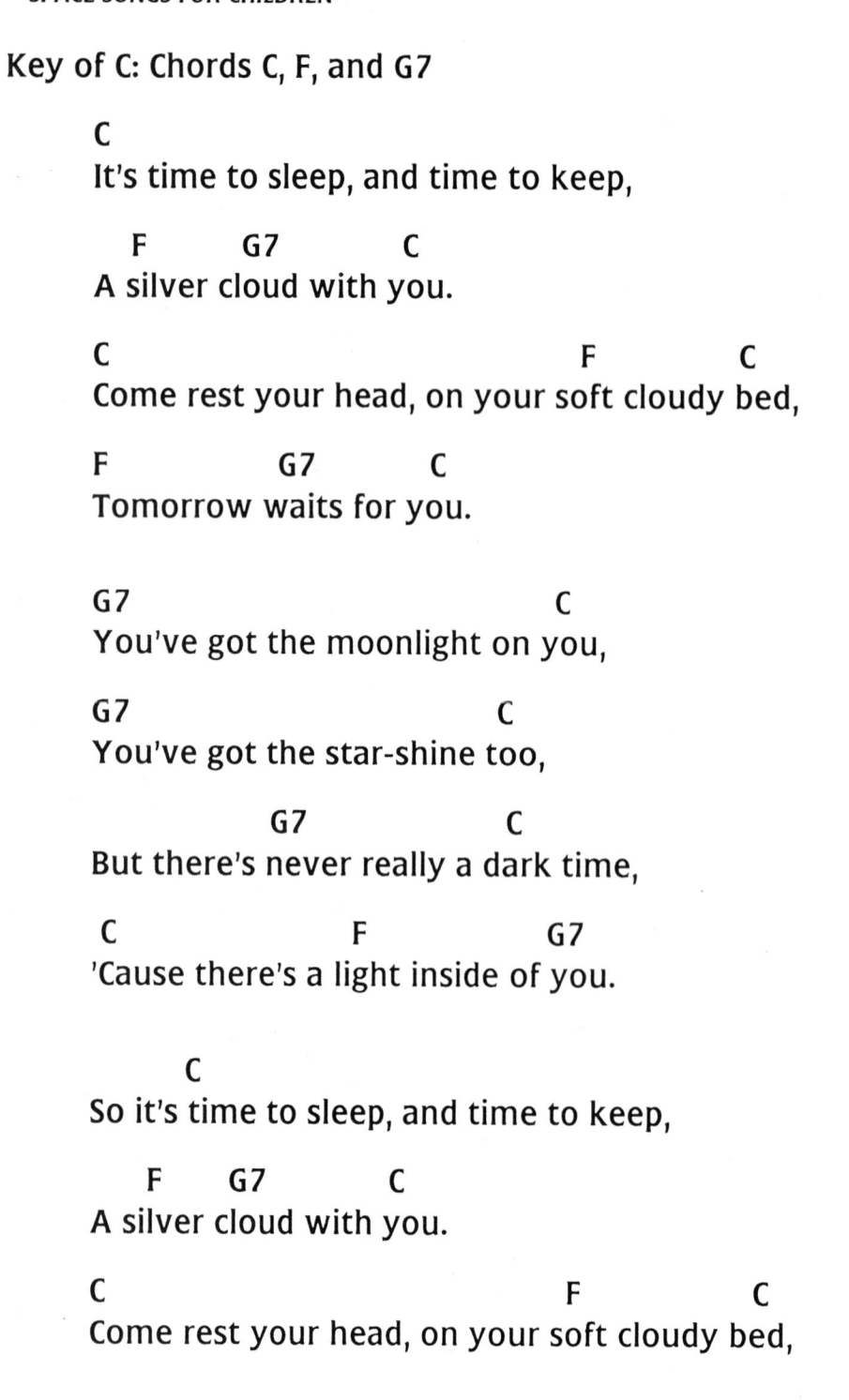

SPACE SONGS FOR CHILDREN

Key of C: Chords C, F, and G7

C
It's time to sleep, and time to keep,

   F   G7   C
A silver cloud with you.

C   F   C
Come rest your head, on your soft cloudy bed,

F   G7   C
Tomorrow waits for you.

G7   C
You've got the moonlight on you,

G7   C
You've got the star-shine too,

        G7   C
But there's never really a dark time,

C   F   G7
'Cause there's a light inside of you.

   C
So it's time to sleep, and time to keep,

   F   G7   C
A silver cloud with you.

C   F   C
Come rest your head, on your soft cloudy bed,

F	G7	C

Tomorrow waits for you,

F	G7	C

Tomorrow waits for you.

Activities or Song Extenders:

- Have children draw a picture of their own sleeping time, whether at home or in their day care setting, school or baby-sitter's. Younger children can dictate to the care-giver what they want to say about their picture. Older children can write their own story. Every family within every culture has certain traditions at bed-time. Encourage children to talk about their home rituals.

- Discuss how the astronauts sleep in space. (They sleep in a sleeping bag, vertically, or horizontally. They have to be strapped in or they will float off. Use pictures and books to show the children what it looks like.) Have the children take turns resting in a sleeping bag, to simulate the astronauts' sleeping time. Have a "sleeping bag" day when children bring their own bags into class to rest in. Have extras for those children who do not have one.

- Have children make and wear a sleeping mask. Discuss how it is daylight every forty-five minutes in the spaceship, and the astronauts need a mask to keep the light out so they can sleep.

- During play time, children can put their favorite doll or stuffed animal in a sleeping bag and "strap it down" so it won't float off, while it is in the spaceship. Have the children sing this lullaby to their doll, or play it for them while they put their dolls to bed in their sleeping bag.

To explore the concept of clouds, do some of the following activities:

- Go outside and observe the clouds in the sky. Do this each day for a week. See if the children can notice the different shapes of the clouds.

- Start to keep a cloud "diary" book. Make a note of how the clouds look each day. Read the diary to the children each day before you go out and look at the clouds. This activity will start to build their awareness of what is going on in the sky.

- Draw pictures of the clouds after you have observed them. Young children can use cotton and glue to make cloud pictures, if they cannot yet draw descriptive pictures.

- Begin to discuss what clouds are really made of, which will lead you to the following experiment:

Children will be able to see how water vapor forms.

Materials or ingredients are a glass bottle, ice cubes and hot water. Follow this procedure:

1. Fill the bottle with hot water.

2. Pour out most of the water, leaving 1 inch of water.

3. Set the bottle in a bright light.

4. Hold an ice cube over the opening.

5. Observe what happens. (A thin cloud will move around in the bottle. This is how water vapor and clouds are formed.)

- Discuss how some clouds might look darker than others on some days. If there is a dark or thicker cloud, it probably means it is going to rain because it has more moisture in it.

- The following information is from the book, "All Aboard For Space," from the Education and Awareness Branch, Kennedy Space Center, Florida, 1992. (See "Resource Centers.")

"There are no clouds in space; however, it is very important to learn about them if you are going to travel in air or space because a pilot can't tell if he is up or down when he flies into a cloud. Cumulus clouds are near the Earth's surface or can tower thousands of feet in the sky. Stratus clouds form in layers like fog and are seldom above 6,500 feet. Cirrus clouds are in the top level of the atmosphere (troposphere) which is below 50,000 feet. Space is above the Earth's atmosphere (troposphere), where there is no moisture or air that is needed to form clouds."

You may want to explain these concepts and vocabulary words to your children, depending on their age and maturity. Use the resource guide to further enhance your knowledge.

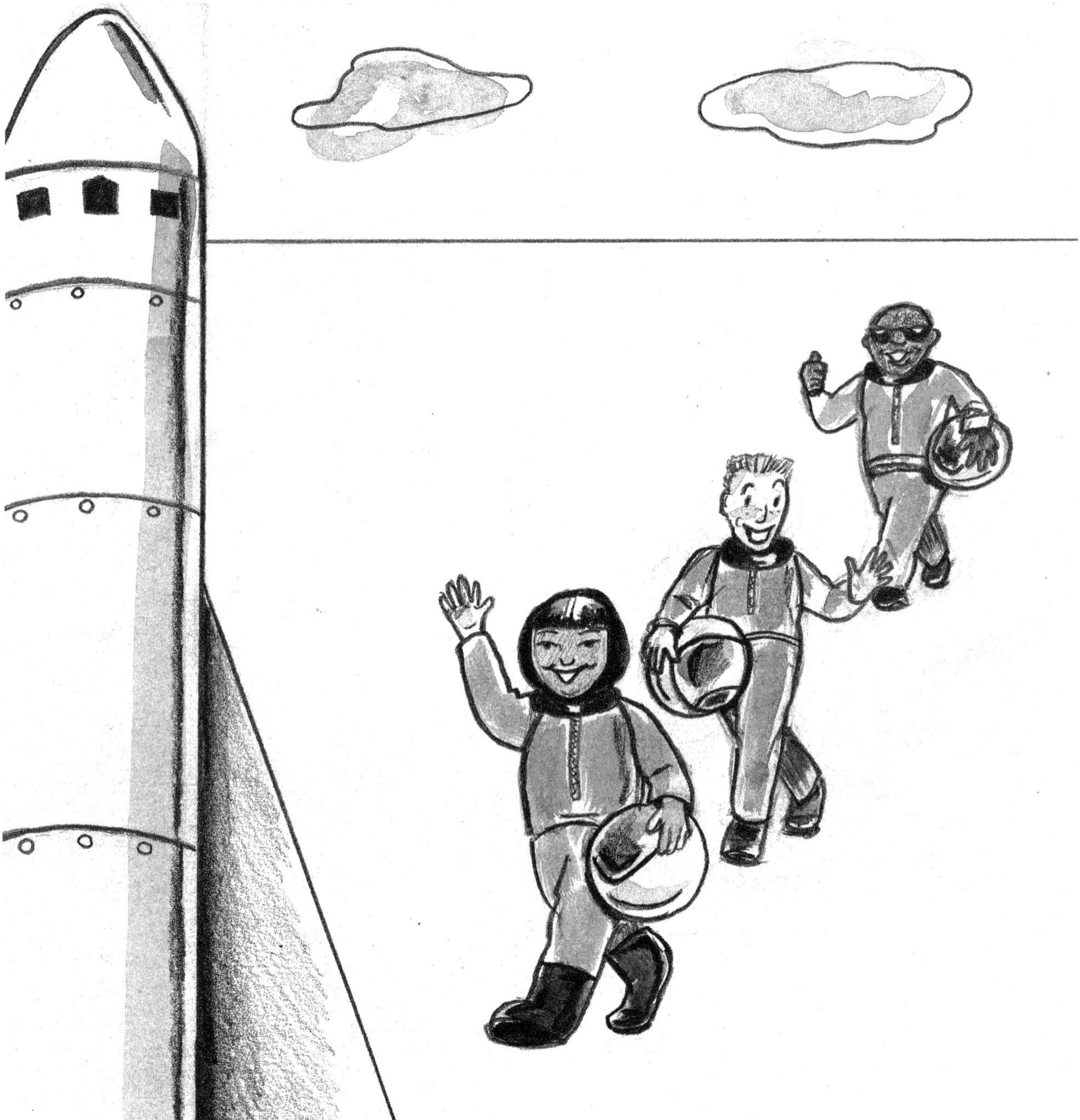

7.

GET ON BOARD

*Traditional; adaptation
by Tonja Evetts Weimer*

This song is about boarding the spacecraft to be launched into outer space. It is also effective when used in a group setting of children, as a transition from one activity to another. It helps build the self-esteem of the children when they hear their names sung. The names sung here are those of some of the astronauts. Depending on the age and maturity of your children, you may want to explain who they are and what missions they flew.

Key of C: Chords C, F, and G7

   C
I have a friend that you all know,

   C
And Robert is his name.

   C
I have a friend that you all know,

   F   G7   C
And Robert is his name.

Chorus

   C   F
So get on board, my friends,

        C
Get on board, my friends,

      F
Get on board, my friends,

    G7   C
There's room for many more.

    G7   C
(This spaceship is ready to fly.)

(Substitute student or astronaut names, i.e., Fred, Jim, John, Mae, Marsha, Brewster)

After singing all the names, the last line of the chorus is:

This spaceship is ready to fly.

These names were selected to acknowledge the following astronauts:

John Glenn	Launches: Mercury Program, Friendship 7, Feb 20, 1962 (U.S. Senator)
Robert Sieck	Launch Director
Robert Crippen	Launches: STS-1, April 12 - 14, 1981; STS-7, June 18 - 24, 1983; 41-C, April 6 - 13, 1984; 41-G, October 5 - 13, 1984.
Fred Gregory	Launches: 51-B, April 29 - May 6, 1985; STS-33, November 22 -27, 1989; STS-44, Nov. 24 - Dec. 1, 1991
Jim Voss	Launches: STS-44, Nov. 24 - Dec. 1, 1991; STS-53, December 2 - 9, 1992.
Mae Jemison	Launch: STS-47, September 12 - 20, 1992.
Marsha Ivins	Launches: STS-32, January 9 - 20, 1990; STS-46, July 31 - Aug 18, 1992.
Brewster Shaw	Launches: 61-B, November 26 -Dec 3, 1985; STS-28, August 8 -13, 1989.

Activities or Song Extenders:

- Sing each child's name to get on board your pretend spacecraft. If you have more than ten children, sing some of the names at the beginning of the exercise, and some at the end. Do not make children wait too long for a turn, or they become bored and restless.

- Show pictures of some of the launches, and tell the children some of the names of the astronauts, and the names of the launches. Change the names in the song to fit the names of the astronauts in the launch picture you have.

- Design and build a spacecraft out of blocks or card board boxes. Paint the spacecraft if it is made of cardboard, and give it a name. Design a logo to suit the name. Children may want to choose a name of one of the astronauts to write on the logo, or on the outside of the spaceship, along with their own name.

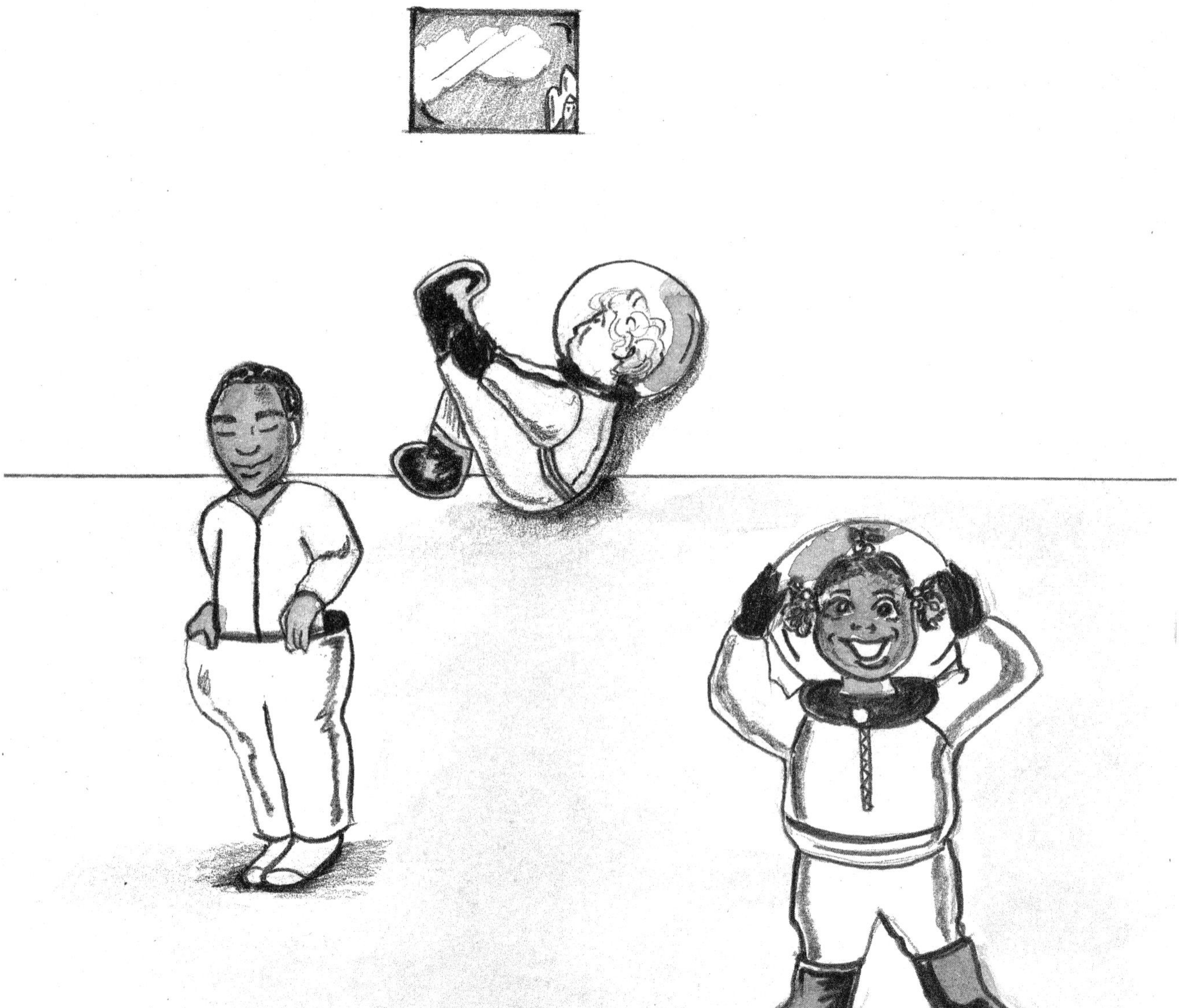

8.

THE MILKY WAY

*Tune: Turkey In The Straw;
words and adaptation
by Tonja Evetts Weimer*

This song introduces the correct titles for the astronauts and the jobs they have when they are on board the spacecraft. It also introduces what the astronauts wear when they ride in the spacecraft and when they walk in space.

Verse, Key of C: Chords C, F, and G7

Chorus, Key of G: Chords G, C, and D7

    C
Well, I woke up before the break of day,

                             G7
And I said "Let's go to the Milky Way."

      C
So I jumped into my astronaut suit,

                      G7   C
And as the commander, this is what I'll do:

(Change Keys)

    G
I'll put on my helmet, put on my suit,

    C
Snap it and zip it, and pull on my boots.

    G   C   D7
Fly 'em up, fly 'em up, high and away,

    G   D7   G
Today is the day for the Milky Way.

(Back to Key of C for the next verse)

Repeat using pilot, mission specialist, and payload specialist in place of commander.

Activities and Song Extenders:

- Have children dramatize getting dressed for space as they sing this song. Discuss why spacesuits are necessary for the astronauts. (It is dark and cold in outer space. There is no air to breathe, and no water to drink.)

- Have a "space helmet" day. Children can bring to school any helmet they have at home such as football, skating, hockey, or bicycle helmets. Discuss why they are needed for safety in sports and why they are needed in space.

- Have a pretend rocket (could be an empty carton formed into the shape of a rocket, or an empty barrel – just make sure it's safe) and have children put on their helmets and pretend to blast off.

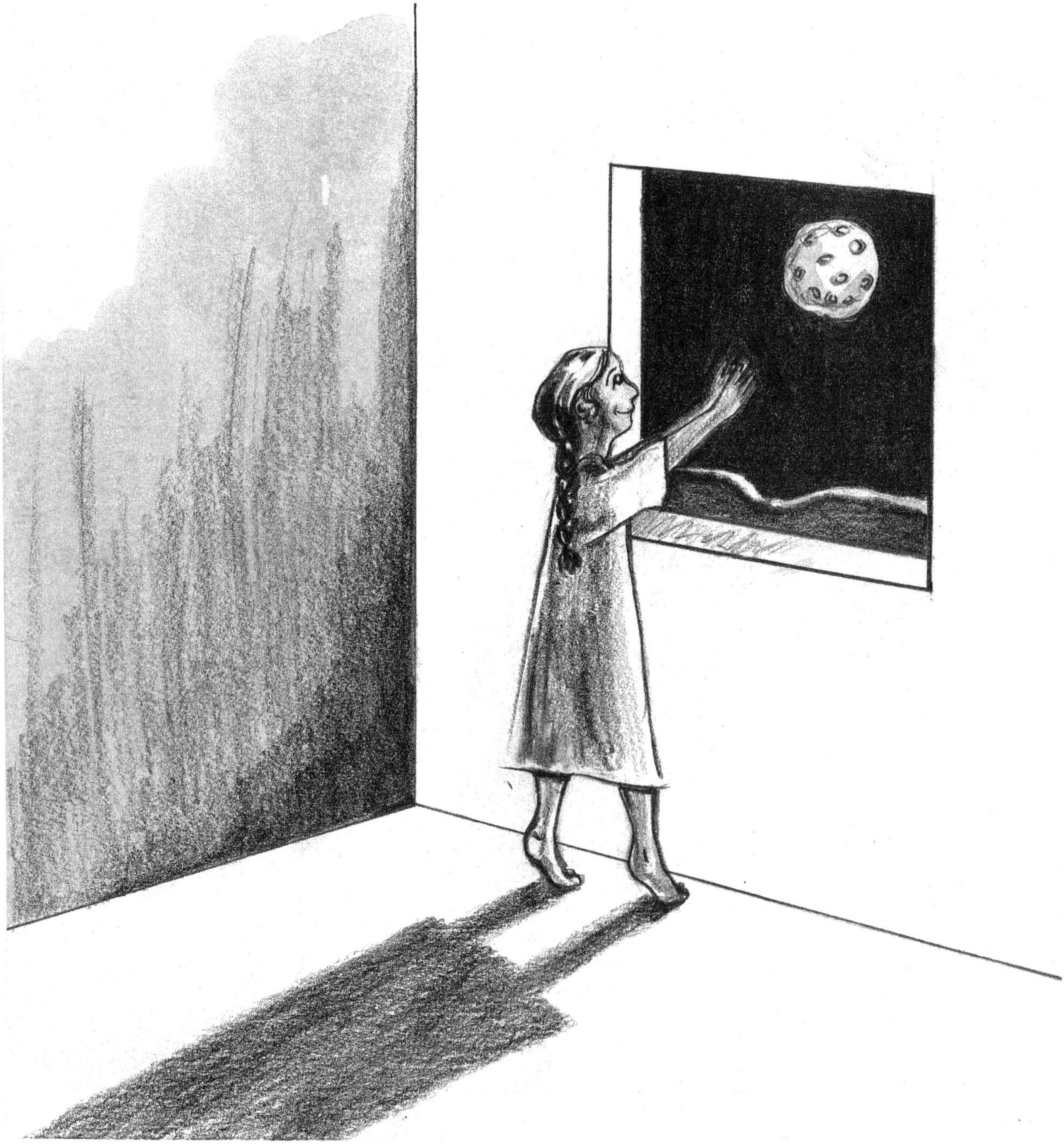

9.

I LOVE MY MOON

*Words and music
by Tonja Evetts Weimer*

The moon is a universal symbol in every culture. It is something that we all share, and many people in many cultures use it as a connecting tie when they are separated from someone they love.

Key of C: Chords C, F, and G7

Verse

```
C                        F    G7
The moon is a great big silver ball,

G7            C
Hanging in the sky.

C              F       G7
But when I try to play with it,

G7              C
I can't reach up that high.
```

Chorus

```
C            F
But oh I love my moon so,

    G7           C
It makes me think of you,

C                 F
And when you look up in the sky,

       G7         C
Maybe you'll think of me too.
```

Verse

```
    C                   F    G7
The moon is a rocky, bumpy place,

G7                    C
Without any grass or trees.

    C                   F    G7
It has no cats and it has no dogs,

G7                      C
And it doesn't have any fleas.
```

Chorus...

Verse

```
    C                F    G7
The moon is like a piece of cheese,

G7           C
Floating over-head.

    C              F    G7
It's yellow and it's full of holes,

G7                     C
But you can't eat it with bread.
```

Chorus...

Activities or Song Extenders:

- Ask children open-ended questions like: 1) "What do you know about the moon?" 2) "What do you like about it?" 3) "Do you know any stories about the moon?" 4) "What does it look like or remind you of?" Encourage discussion and accept all answers. If we truly accept children's thoughts, they will open up and contribute more.

- Use this discussion as the introduction to finding out more about the moon. Take children to the library and check out books about the moon, the solar system and space. Play the song again, and ask who would like to do a "Moon Dance"? Pretend to be dancing on the moon. Flowing scarves or crepe paper streamers may be used as "props" to get the children into the softness of this dance. Tell the children to make the streamer "dance".

- Explain that the United States was the first country to put a man on the moon. No plants, animals or water were found on the moon. There were only hills, valleys of rocks, and plains of light gray soil.

- † Talk about the different shapes of the moon. Explain that the moon is always round, but sometimes we see only part of it. With children five and older, make a poster showing the different phases of the moon. Help the children label the different phases accurately. Use these terms:

- full moon ... refers to complete side of moon being illuminated.

- gibbous ... more than half but less than full.

- crescent ... less than half but more than a quarter.

- quarter ... first or last quarter

- † Teach children how to do "Moon Shouting." Explain to the children that sounds cannot be heard on the moon. (The moon has no air so sounds can't travel.)

Have the children all shout as loud as they can. (You may want to do this outside, using "outside" voices.) When the children have finished shouting, show them how to pretend to shout without making sounds. Encourage them to try it. Tell them it is called "moon shouting," because their shout could not be heard on the moon. You might find that moon shouting is so much fun, it makes a good transition before a story or circle activity.

---

† From: "A Resource Unit for the Moon," Texas Child Care Quarterly, Fall 1988, by Linda Ard. (Used with permission.)

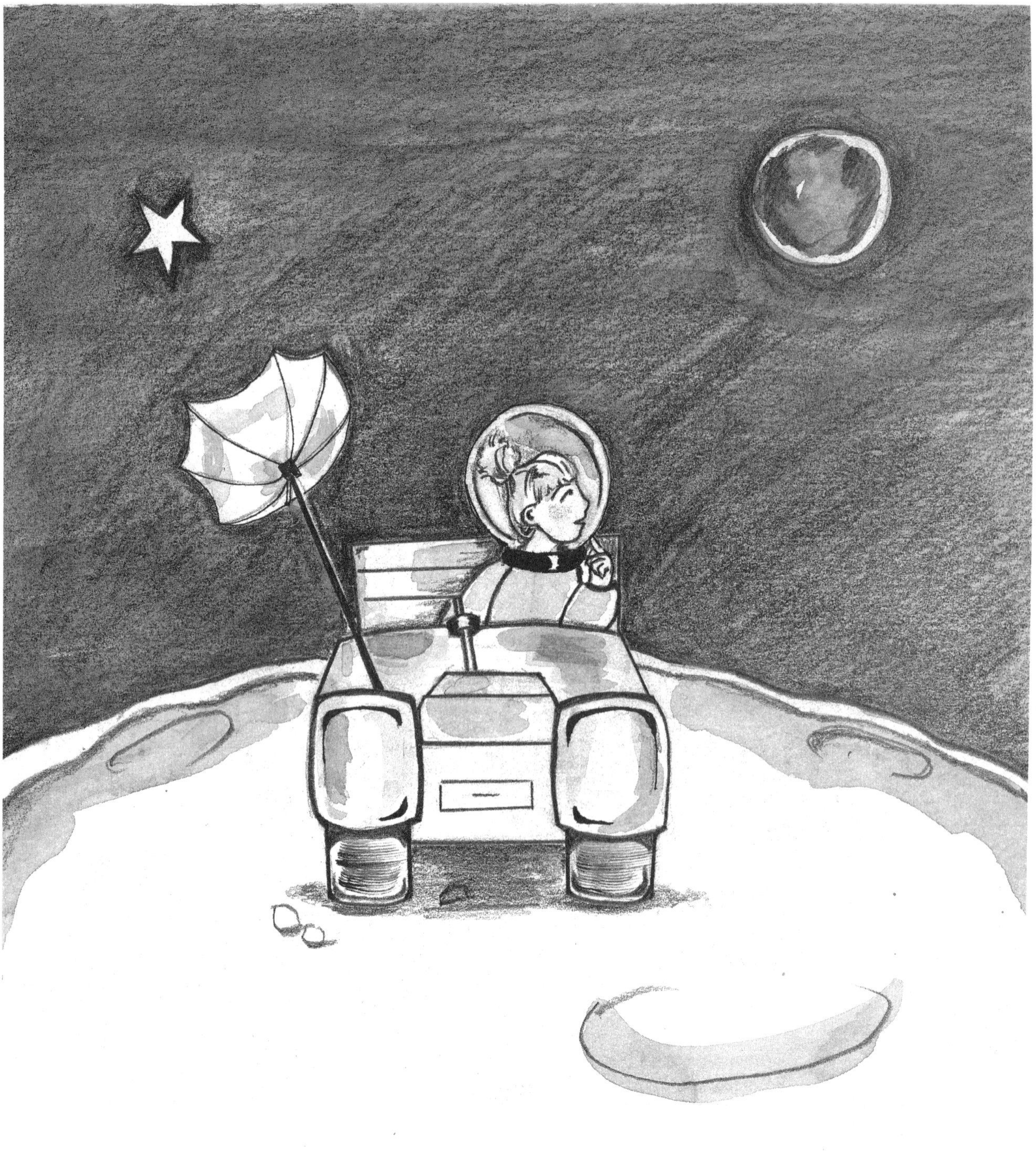

10.

RIDING IN MY SPACE BUGGY

Tune: Riding in the Buggy, Miss Mary Jane;
Traditional folk song from South Carolina.
Words and adaptation
by Tonja Evetts Weimer

This song introduces the lunar rover, also known as a space buggy, designed to be driven on the moon. Children can dramatize driving it.

Key of C: Chords C, F, and G7

Verse

    C
Riding in my space buggy, bumping along,

      G7   C
I'm bumping along, bumping along,

    C
Riding in my space buggy, bumping along,

      F   G7 C
I'm a long way from home...

Chorus

    C   F   C
Who misses me? Who misses me?

    C   G7   C
Who misses me, Oh Mama, who misses me?

Verse

    C
Riding in my lunar rover, picking up rocks,

      G7   C
I'm picking up rocks, picking up rocks.

C
Riding in my lunar rover, picking up rocks,

    F   G7   C
I'm a long way from home.

Chorus...

C   F   C
Who misses me? Who misses me?

C   G7   C
Who misses me, Oh Mama, who misses me?

Verse

C
Riding in my space ship, I'm flying home,

G7   C
Flying home, flying home.

C
Riding in my space ship, I'm flying home,

    F   G7 C
I've a long way to go,

To see ...

Chorus...

```
C                F            C
Who misses me?  Who misses me?

C                              G7           C
Who misses me, Oh Mama, who misses me?
```

Activities or Song Extenders:

- Discuss how the astronauts collected rock specimens and brought them back to Earth, when they went to the moon.

  These rocks can be seen at various space museums around the United States.

- Take a "rock walk" and gather some rocks for your science area. Look at them with a magnifying glass. Describe how they look and feel. Sort and classify them by weight, shape, color, size, texture, etc. Let children classify them with a blindfold on, once they understand the comparisons that can be done by feeling them.

- Children can look at the sand in the sand box or on the ground outdoors after a hard, short rain. It may look like the surface of the moon with pits and holes. This can give them the idea of a bumpy surface.

- To have another experience of the moon's surface, fill a pan with plaster of Paris. Drop rocks of different sizes into it and then remove them. The holes they make will look similar to moon craters. Form some mounds and flat spaces, and sprinkle with dry dirt. This simulates the rest of the surface of the moon (mountains and plains). Have pictures of the moon on the walls for the children to see, to extend their concept of the moon's surface.

- Go to the library and check out some of the books about the moon that are listed in the bibliography. "The Moon Ride Rock Hunt" by Margaret Friskey will answer many questions the children might have.

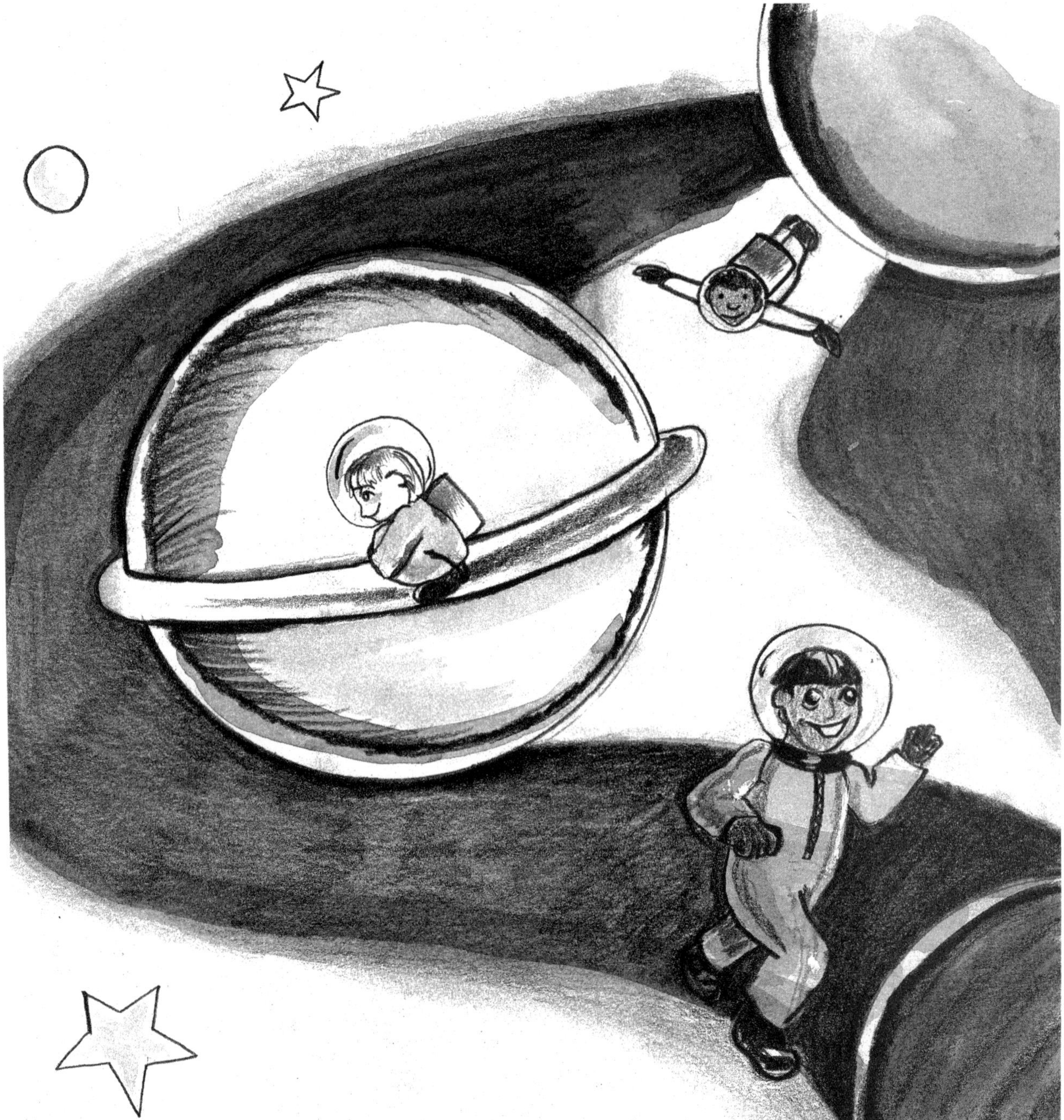

11.

JUMPING TO JUPITER

*Tune: Going to Boston;
Traditional folk song;
words and adaptation
by Tonja Evetts Weimer*

This song is to teach the names of the planets. Children may not be able to grasp the distance to the planets, nor can they see them in the sky, but like the study of dinosaurs, they are able to learn and remember their names and distinguishing characteristics. Singing and doing the actions to the songs will aid in remembering the names of the planets, also.

Key of G: Chords G, C, and D7
Key of C: Chords C, F, and G7

   G   C
Come on children, jump to Jupiter,

   D7   G
Come on children, jump to Jupiter,

   G   C
Come on children, jump to Jupiter,

   D7   G
Er-lie in the morning.

Repeat, using motions with planet names:

Come on children, float to Mercury,...

Come on children, walk to Venus,...

Come on children, roll to Mars,...

(Change to key of C)

   C   F
Come on children, jog to Saturn,

```
G7                    C
```
Come on children, jog to Saturn,

```
C                     F
```
Come on children, jog to Saturn,

```
G7          C
```
Er-lie in the morning.

Come on children, fly to Uranus,…

Come on children, dance to Neptune,…

Come on children, sing to Pluto,…

Come on children, back to Earth (Come sit down).

Activities or Song Extenders:

- The planets are made more real to children by hanging a mobile of them and discussing what each one looks like, and how it is different from the others. A mobile can be constructed from various sizes of styrofoam balls.

- Explain that planets are different from stars in that they travel in orbit, rotate on their axes, are not gaseous, and do not give off heat and light. They reflect light from the sun. A star is a fixed body, is gaseous and gives off heat and light.

- All of the planets are sung in this song. Refer to pictures of the solar system as you sing it.

- Have the children dramatize the solar system by being the sun and the planets. Have one child be the sun, and have the other children be the planets, revolving around the sun. This gives the children a real, tangible experience of the concept of rotation, and how our solar system moves. They can also see where the Earth is in relation to the sun, and the other planets.

The following information is quoted from "All Aboard For Space," Education and Awareness Branch, Kennedy Space Center, Florida. 1992 (see Resources)

"The Space Shuttle and NASA satellites are exploring our solar system. The sun is the center of our solar system and the planets revolve around the sun. Space probes (satellites) have visited other planets. Pictures of the planets can be obtained from NASA.

Mercury: Closest to the sun; yellow in color; life as we know it isn't possible because there is no air or water and it's too hot or too cold, depending on which direction it is facing.

Venus: Closest to the size of the Earth; life isn't possible as we know it; we call it our morning or evening star.

Earth: The only planet that has life on it; one moon; length of each day is twenty-four hours.

Mars: Two Viking spacecraft landed on Mars in July and September, 1976, found rolling dunes of orange dust and volcanic rocks; water may have been on Mars about a billion years ago or may be underground; took many exciting photographs and performed many experiments.

Jupiter: Pioneers 10 and 11 spacecraft visited Jupiter March, 1972 and April, 1973; discovered rings; largest planet with 16 moons.

Saturn: Voyager spacecraft verified 18 - 21 moons and over 1000 rings on a recent visit to Saturn.

Uranus: The Uranus Encounter, by Voyager II, discovered ten additional satellites, bringing the total number of satellites (moons) to fifteen, verified ten rings around Uranus; green in color.

Neptune: Voyager II spacecraft visited Neptune last; has two moons that go in opposite directions.

Pluto: Orbit is inside Neptune until 1999; one moon called Charon."

Consult the Bibliography for more books and resources about the planets.

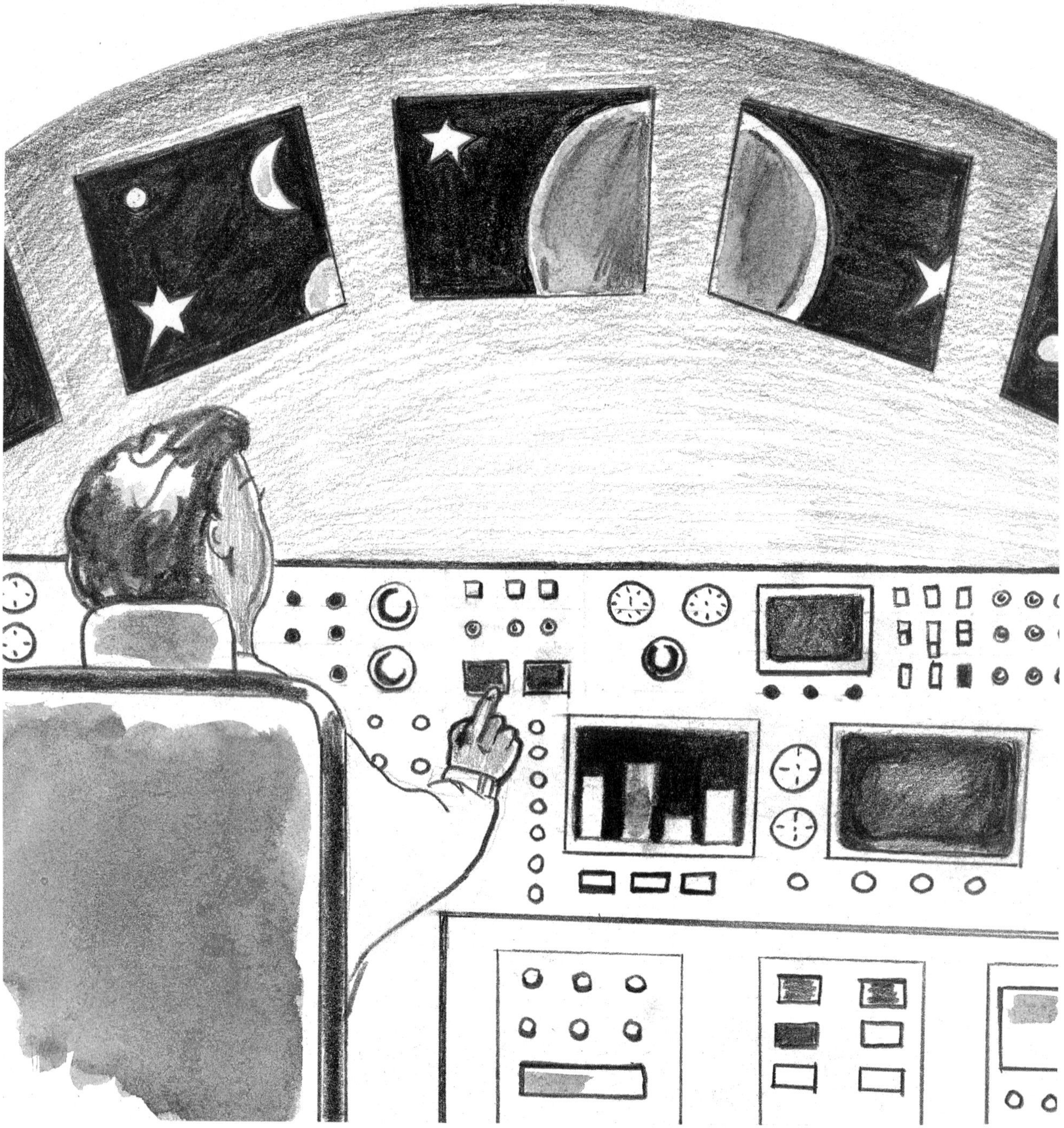

12.

LITTLE WINDOWS

*Words and music
by Tonja Evetts Weimer*

This song introduces the child to the feeling of being inside a spacecraft. The windows were very small in the original spaceships, and today, airplanes also give children a feeling of "little windows." Use this song as a rest song for nap time or bed time.

Key of C: Chords C, F, and G7

Verse

    C   G7
Looking out my little windows,

G7   C
Looking down upon the Earth,

    C   G7
Looking out my little windows,

G7   C
Sleeping in my little berth.

Chorus

    C   F
Flying in my little spaceship,

      G7   C
As the world goes by so fast,

    C   F
Looking out my little windows,

      G7   C
Looking down upon my past.

Verse

```
    C               G7
Pushing all the little buttons,

G7                  C
Checking all the little lights,

    C               G7
Watching all the screens before me,

                    C
Thinking of the many nights
```

Chorus

```
    C                    F
That I went flying in my spaceship,

        G7              C
As the world goes by so fast...
```

(Rest of Chorus)

Verse

```
    C                G7
How I love my little windows,

G7                   C
I can see the nights and days,
```

    C   G7
I can see the stars a twinkling,

    G7   C
I can see the sun a blaze.

Chorus

    C   F
Flying in my little spaceship, etc.

Activities or Song Extenders:

- This song opens up for discussion the thoughts and feelings of looking down on the Earth as one would fly overhead. Use a globe or a ball with the Earth on it to look down on when children are in their pretend spacecraft.

- Using cardboard boxes and crayons, design the inside of a spaceship, with the little windows, screens, and many buttons to push. If your children have the opportunity to ride on an airplane, or visit an airport, try to arrange a visit to the cockpit. This will give them some idea of "all the little buttons."

- Use crepe paper streamers, flowing scarves, ribbons or flowing material as props to dance with to this music. Tell the children to make the "streamer" dance through the spaces of high, middle, and low. Soon, the children will be using more of their bodies to express their dance to the music.

Concluding Activities:

Teachers: Have children draw pictures of their favorite song(s). When you have finished doing all of the activities from the album, have your whole group of children make a class mural. Label each child's drawing, with their name. For individual pictures, write on the picture what they want to tell about it. Older children will be able to write their own sentences.

Keep a journal of what children say as you do some or all of these activities. Have the journal available for parents to look through when they visit.

The children may enjoy singing some of the songs for the parents and acting them out. Encourage the children to share with their parents what they have learned about outer space.

Parents: You may want to keep a diary of your children's comments and observations about space and the related activities. Save your children's drawings also. The children will want to see their art work and read their own comments when they are older. Be sure and put their ages and the dates on all of their work or comments.

Both parents and teachers may want to tape-record or video-tape the children doing many of the space song activities. Photographs of the child in space costume, or of the space vehicle they built will be treasured. Put labels on these pictures to stimulate reading and language development. Put the pictures with their captions around the room, on the walls, or on a table. The child may look at them often, and retell the events or read them to friends.

The space song activities were created to promote learning through all of the senses, as well as "learning by doing." When children are taught in this way, their retention is likely to be much higher, and their learning experience more positive and meaningful.

BIBLIOGRAPHY AND RESOURCES

Glossary of Space Terms
Reprinted from Texas Child Care Quarterly, Fall 1988

Astronaut – a person who trains for and goes on flights into space.

Craters – round holes on the moon's surface. They are caused by chunks of rock called meteorites smashing into the moon. Some are no bigger than pin holes but most are the size of a big lake (5 to 10 miles wide).

Earth – the place we live. It is a huge ball of rock. It floats in space and moves around the sun. It is called a planet.

Gravity – the downward pull of the earth or any heavenly body on objects or people. Gravity holds us down on Earth. Spacecraft must travel fast to get free of gravity. There is no gravity in space. Everything floats. (Ask a child to hold a wooden block in one hand with the arm extended straight. Soon the block will feel heavy, and the child will want to put the arm down. The arm is being pulled down by the Earth's gravity.)

Impact – when two things hit against each other such as the jolt of a rock landing on a sidewalk.

Launching pad – the special surface where a spacecraft is shot up from the Earth into space. A rocket called a Saturn V was used to shoot most of the Apollo spacecraft into space on trips to the moon. (Children can try launching balls into space by throwing them up as high as possible.)

Lift-off – the sudden upward movement of a spacecraft when it takes off.

Meteoroid – a chunk of rock that moves around the sun through space. When one hits the moon or Earth, it is called a meteorite.

Orbit – the circular path around an object such as the moon's path around the Earth. A satellite or spacecraft is held in orbit by the pull of gravity. The path can be controlled by the speed of the spacecraft and the angle of the launch. (To help children understand an orbit, fasten a string to a tennis ball and have a child whirl the ball overhead. The ball moves only in a circle, and the string is like the pull of gravity.)

Oxygen – part of the air we breathe. You can't see, smell, or taste it, but all living things need it to live. (Air also contains nitrogen, hydrogen, and carbon dioxide.) The earth is wrapped by a layer of air called the atmosphere.

Phases – the changes in the moon. The phases are called quarter, crescent, gibbous, and full. Because the moon has no light of its own, we see only the part that the sun shines on. It takes about 29 days for the moon to go around the Earth, so we see a full moon about once a month.

Reflection – what happens when light, heat, or sound bounces off a surface. A piece of aluminum foil held toward the sun reflects light and heat. A mirror reflects light and heat. A mirror reflects an image. The moon does not shine by itself but rather reflects the sun's light.

Rocket – the part of a spacecraft that shoots it into space. Most of a rocket is made up of fuel; when it is burned up, the rocket cannot be used any more. (To help children understand how a rocket works, blow up a balloon without knotting it and let it go. It will fly away as air rushes out.)

Satellite – manmade or natural (like the moon) objects that travel about the Earth in an orbit. We use satellites to take pictures of clouds and their movements so that we can learn about weather conditions. Satellites can sometimes be seen in the sky on a clear night.

Space – everything beyond the clouds. It goes on forever. The sun, moon, stars, meteoroids, and our Earth are in space.

Spacecraft – any satellite or spaceship that travels into space.

Space shuttle – a rocket plane that takes off by a rocket and lands on an airplane runway. Unlike earlier spacecraft, the shuttle can be used many times. It can take people from Earth to space stations.

Space station – a spacecraft where people can live and work for several months. It circles the Earth and can be used to launch other spacecraft. The first space station was the American Skylab.

Tides – the movement of the oceans caused by the moon's gravity tugging at the Earth. There are two high tides and two low tides each day, changing every six hours. You can see the changes in the tides by observing how far the waves come up on the beach or piers.

Supplemental Materials

1. **Space Sponges for art work.** Ten one inch thick sponges are cut into shapes of astronauts, stars, moon, rockets and planets. $10.00 From Environments, Inc., P.O. Box 1348, Beaufort Industrial Park, Beaufort, S.C. 29901-1348. Call 1-800-EI-CHILD.

2. **Hug-A-Planets** are soft globes that show countries, continents and oceans. Cotton/polyester with shredded foam. Large 12" globe $15.85; Small 6" globe $8.80. Environments, Inc.

3. **The inflatable plastic shuttle** is available from Myra Halpin and Assoc., 605 Hammond, Durham, NC 27701. $49.95, including text. Children can role play living in space.

4. For space appropriate clothes and products, write for the following catalogs:
   * Civil Air Patrol Bookstore, Bldg 749, Maxwell AFB, AL 36112.
   * Aviator Country, Box 181, 1216 Forth Rd., Lyons, WI 53148.

   Other products can be purchased from NASA gift shops, and Space Port USA at the Kennedy Space Center, FL.

5. Children can build space stations with Lego Land Space Systems models. The surface rover and astronauts and space station kits are available at most toy stores.

6. From Environments (1-800-EI-CHILD), the following materials are artistic in design, and create a festive mood of sky and space for young children:

   Day and Night Banners, set of 3, 74.00
   Sky Banners, four 18" X 48", 56.00
   Space Banners, set of three, 18" X 36", 125.00
   Down to Earth Mat, world floor mat, five foot diameter, 1" thick, soft foam, 115.00

7. **Space Shuttle**, from Constructive Playthings, is a complete set of durable plastic pieces. It has an elevator, mission control center, flat bed tractor, fuel truck, two all-terrain-vehicles, booster rockets, and five astronauts dressed for take-off. (1-800-448-4115) 29.95

8. Creative School House has two puzzles about space. One is by Lauri, is a space-ship, 25 pieces, and is made of crepe foam rubber. The other is made by Judy, is an astronaut, and has 13 pieces. 806-796-2975.

Annotated Bibliography
Children's Books
Relating To Aviation and Space

Franklin M. Branley. New York: Thomas Y. Crowell Co. Series of children's books on all aerospace topics with simple text, delightfully illustrated:

The Big Dipper

A Book of Outer Space

A Book of Planets (Describes each of the nine planets)

A Book of Satellites

A Book of Flying Saucers for You (Discusses sightings of flying saucers or UFOs with possible explanations)

Eclipse: Dark in Daytime

Gravity is a Mystery

Is There Life in Outer Space?

Journey into a Black Hole

The Moon Seems to Change (New York: Harper and Row 1987) (The phases of the moon are described.)

The Moon-Jack and Jill and Other Legends (Lexington MA: Ginn and Co 1972) (Legends of the moon and the phases are explained.)

North South East and West (Beginners learn to tell directions to locate directions with gravity map reading and compass reading activities.)

The Planets in Our Solar System (Introduction of the solar system with directions for making models of the relative sizes and distances)

Rockets and Satellites (Explains a rocket and satellite functions)

BIBLIOGRAPHY AND RESOURCES

Saturn (Describes the 6th planet from the sun its rings and moons with photographs)

The Sky is Full of Stars

The Sun-Our Nearest Star (Explains the sun is a star with examples of how large and hot the sun is)

Sunshine Makes the Seasons

Weight and Weightlessness

What Makes Day and Night

What the Moon is Like (Description of sights and experiences on the moon based on information gathered from astronauts)

A Day in Space. Suzanne Lord and Jolie Epstein. New York: Scholastic Books, Inc., 1986. (A factual book detailing an astronaut's training and a space flight using actual NASA photographs. All aspects of the flight are covered- eating, sleeping, working and playing with the toys in space.)

Airplanes, Spaceships and Balloons. Sue Swallow. New York: MacDonald and Co., 1974. (Simple encyclopedia for very young readers including pages on planes, gliding, airships and the moon.)

Amelia's Flying Machine. Barbara Shook Hazen, New York: Doubleday and Co., 1977. (A young girl spends the summer with her grandmother and cousins. They have many adventures, one of which was building a flying machine.)

All About the Stars. Anne Terry White. New York: Random House, 1954. (The stars as seen and understood by scientists)

Anansi, The Spider. Gerald McDermott. New York: Holt, Rinehart and Winston, 1972. (In trying to determine which of his six sons to reward for saving his life, Anansi, the spider, is responsible for placing the moon in the sky.)

The Ant and the Astronaut. A. Mityayev. Moscow Progress Publishers, 1973. (This is a story about an ant who is the only member of his colony to have the honor of talking with an astronaut. The other stories in the book discuss gravity, night and day, a meteor shower and the atmosphere.)

Angry Moon. Sleator Johnson. Boston: Little, 1970. (Northwest Coast Native American story about the angry moon man being outwitted by a magic spell and devotion of a small boy.)

Around the World in Ninety Minutes: The Journey of Two Astronauts. Rocco V. Feravoio. New York: Lothrop, Lee & Shepard, Co, Inc., 1968. (The author takes the reader from the landing pad, through a journey and back to earth.)

Astronauts. Carol Green. Chicago: Children's Press, 1984. (The discussion of space travel from the beginning to the present. Training and duties of the astronauts are discussed.)

The Astronauts. Dinah L. Moche. New York: Random House, 1978. (Actual photos depict the astronauts jobs and their space ships.)

Astronaut Critter. Mercer Mayer. New York: Little, Simon, 1986. (Astronaut Critter makes a space ship to take him into space. He takes pictures, eats a snack, looks at the moon and more. During the story, you realize Space Critter is still on the ground using his imagination.)

Beyond the Milky Way. Cecile Schoberle. New York: Crown, 1986. (Looking out a city window and seeing the night sky between the buildings, a child describes the glowing wonder of outer space and imagines another child doing the same on a distant planet.)

Book of Greek Myths. Ingri and Edgar Parin d'Aulaire. Garden City, New York: Doubleday, 1962. (The Greek myth describing Helios, the sun, as a flaming charioteer who speeds his fiery steeds across the sky and Selene, the moon, his quiet sister who drives her white horses nightly across the sky.)

BIBLIOGRAPHY AND RESOURCES

The Challenge of Space. Robin Kerrod. Minneapolis: Lerner Publications Co., 1980. (A question and answer book about rockets, satellites and space travel.)

Come to Work with Us in Aerospace. Jean Wilkinson and Ned Wilkinson. Milwaukee, Wisconsin: Sextant Systems, 1970. (Children take adult jobs, all of which deal with the aerospace industry. Each page describes a job.)

Comets. Kate Petty. New York: Franklin Watts, 1985. (Non-fiction book explains what comets are and what they look like. Includes information about comets and meteorites seen in the past, such as Halley's Comet. Questions and answers in the back of the book.)

Comets, Asteroids and Meteors. Dennis B. Fradin. Chicago: Children's Press, 1984. (Non-fiction book that discusses the solar systems, comets, asteroids and meteors. Includes vivid color photographs. Also contains a list of some famous comets, the largest asteroids and some yearly meteor showers.)

The Double Planet. Isaac Asimov. London: Abelard-Schuman, 1960. (Scientific study of the earth and moon. Many facts and charts are provided.)

Easy to Make Spaceships That Really Fly. Mary Blocksma and Dewey Blocksma. New Jersey: Englewood Cliffs, 1983. (Displays the different patterns of spaceships that children can make and what materials are needed.)

Emily Emerson Moon. Jean Merfill and Ronnie Solbert. Boston: Little, Brown and Co., 1983. (A rhymed story about a little girl and her father who gets her a sun (a sunflower), a rainbow (a ribbon) and the moon (a reflection in the goldfish pool.)

Far Out How to Create Your Own Star World. Robin West. Minneapolis, Minnesota First Avenue Editions, a division of Lerner Publications Co., 1987. (Kids can create their own star world by using a few easily found household items. Projects such as Astro Shuttle, Interplanetary Rover, Meteor Man and Cosmic Centipede are described.)

Flying. Donald Crews. New York: Greenwillow Books, 1986. (An airplane take-off is described. The plane passes over cities, countries, lakes and more.)

The Galaxies. David Darling. Minneapolis, Minnesota: Dillon Press, 1985. (Galaxies are explained-how they were formed and the types of galaxies.)

The Glorious Flight. Across the Channel with Louis Bleriot. Alice and Martin Provensen. New York: Viking Penguin, Inc., 1983. (A biography of the man whose fascination with flying machines produced the Bleriot XI which in 1909 became the first heavier-than-air machine to fly the English Channel.)

Goodnight Moon. Margaret Wise Brown. New York: Harper and Rowe, 1947. (The classic story of a child's day ending. The moon in the night sky is told goodnight as little rabbit tells about pictures on the walls of his room.)

Great Valentine's Day Balloon Race. Adrienne Adams. New York: McMillan Publishing Co., 1980.

Happy Birthday, Moon. Frank Asch. New Jersey: Eglewood Cliffs, 1982. (A little bear talks to the moon. He imagines that the echoes really respond to him.)

Hiawatha. Henry Wadsworth Longfellow. New York: Dial, 1983. (Eastern Woodland Native American legend about the moon, the Milky Way and rainbows.)

How the Sun Made a Promise and Kept it. Retold by Margery Bernstein and Janet Kobrin. New York: Charles Scribner's Sons, 1974. (Long ago the sun went wherever he wanted to go. Whenever he went away, it became dark and cold. So the god Weeseke-jak decided to catch him, which was a big mistake. The earth became too hot. Finally the beaver released the sun.)

I Feel the Same Way. Lilian Moors. New York: Athenum, 1967. (A book of poetry, depicting nature from a child's point of view.)

I Saw a Rocket Walk a Mile: Nonsense Tales, Chants and Songs From Many lands. Carl A. Withers. New York: Holt, Rinehart and Co., 1965. (Folklore poems that deal with space.)

BIBLIOGRAPHY AND RESOURCES

If I Flew a Plane. Robert Quackenbush. Englewood, New Jersey: Prentice Hall, Inc., 1970. (This story describes a boy's dreams of what he will be when he becomes a man. This time the boy is a future pilot trying to decide what kind of aircraft he will be flying. He tries out various kinds: Passenger, cargo, sport sky writers, spaceships, helicopters and a glider.)

In the Air. Edward Ranisbotton and Joan Redmayne. Cleveland, Ohio: Modern Curriculum Press, 1983. (This open-ended book gives the child activities in reading and thinking.)

Jet Bed. Janis Asad. Cleveland, Ohio: Modern Curriculum Press, Inc., 1981. (A primary reader featuring short vowels. Ken dreams that his bed turns into a jet. He falls off the jet and the web men capture him. They tug at his leg, but then he wakes up to find it is only a dream.)

Jets and Rockets. Barker, Allen. London: Chapman and Hall, 1959. (100 experiments including air is real, air can push, action and reaction, how jet engines develop thrust, the air intake and compression, combustion chamber, the turbine, will jets get to the moon, how rockets work.)

Journey to the Moon. Erich Fuchs. New York: Delacorte Press, 1969. (A wordless picture book of a space flight of Apollo 11, In the front of the book is a narration of the pages.)

Jupiter. Seymour Simon. New York: William Morrow and Co., Inc, 1985. (The book gives a vivid description of the characteristics of the planet Jupiter and its moons shown through photographs sent back to earth by Voyager spaceships.)

Let's Find Out About Space Travel. Martin Shapp and Charles Shapp. New York: Watts Publishers, 1971. (The book highlights the history of man's urge to travel in space. It covers the space flying machine inventions and the first astronauts.)

Little Plane. Michael Gay. New York: Macmillan, 1983. (A story about a little plane as he sets off for a day in the sky. He does somersaults, races with the birds, rests on a cloud and finally returns home for a well-earned night's sleep.)

Many Moons. James Thurber. New York: Harcourt, 1971. (The classic story about the perception of the moon as a small object. The discussion about perception could be introduced.)

The Mars Landing. Leila Boyle Gemme. Chicago: Children's Press, 1977. (Details the exploration of the planet Mars and the landing of the Viking spacecraft with photography that has been beamed back to earth.)

Meteor! Patricia Polacco. New York: Dodd, Mead and Co., 1987. (The children with grampa and gramma were all frightened when something landed in the front lawn. Everyone in the town came to see the meteor. The people who touched it said they felt something magical and special. True story.)

Mission Outer Space. Robin Kerrod. Minneapolis, Minnesota: Lerner Publications Co., 1980. (A question and answer book about space and the planets and man's attempts to learn about them through manned space missions.)

Moon. Gordon Davies. New York: Wonder Books, 1977. (An easy reader book describing the astronauts journey to the moon, their landing and what they did on the moon. The phases of the moon and telescopes are also explained.)

Mooncake. Frank Asch. Englewood Cliffs, New Jersey: Prentice-Hall, 1983. (A small bear builds a rocket to go to the moon, hibernates, and awakes to find himself in unfamiliar snow. He decides it's the moon, returns to hibernation and awakes, none the wiser.)

The Moon Jumpers. Janice May Udry. New York: Harper and Row, 1959. (A description of playing in the moonlight.)

Moon Man. Tomi Ungerel. New York: Harper and Rowe, 1967. (A fantasy picture book about the man-in-the-moon. He comes to the earth, goes through the phases and returns to the moon.)

BIBLIOGRAPHY AND RESOURCES

The Moon Ride Rock Hunt. Margaret Friskey. Chicago: Children's Press, 1972. (A true book of the moonwalk adventure. Photographs and simplified text depict the operations of the Apollo 11 lunar landing.)

My First Book About Space, a question and answer book. Dinah L. Moche. Racine, Wisconsin: Western Publishing Co., Inc., 1982. (An informative book for primary children that tells about things that are different about earth and space.)

My Space Adventure. Karen McGraw Hefty. Milton, Florida: Create A Book, 1982. (This story tells about the planning of a space trip to planet LOVE. The book is personalized with names and places.)

My Trip to the Space Station. Jane Hodges. Edisto Island, South Carolina: Edisto Press, 1987. (This book talks about the NASA astronaut children who want to visit space. They've been taught about things in space and are finally ready to make their first trip. They go into space via a shuttle, visit the space station and use space supplies, play with the toys in space and do experiments in space.)

On the Moon. Angela Grunsell. New York: Franklin Watts, 1983. (Describes Aldrin's, Collins' and Armstrong's trip to the moon and what they did on the moon.)

Other Worlds. David Darling. Minneapolis, Minnesota: Dillon Press, 1985. (Examines the evidence which may support the possibilities of life elsewhere in the universe and discusses the efforts we have made to pick up signals from outer space.)

Parachute Play. Liz and Dick Wilmes. New York: Building Blocks, 1985. (Activities that can be done with outdoor parachute play.)

Race for the Moon. Robin Kerrod. Minneapolis, Minnesota: Lerner Publication, 1980. (A question and answer book about the moon and space missions to the moon. Includes an index of US manned space flights.)

Ready for Take-Off. Robin Lawrie. New York: Pantheon Books, A Division of Random House, Inc., 1971. (The description of how an airplane flies, beginning with a discussion on gravity and how an airplane is able to rise. A plane flight from takeoff to landing.)

Regards to the Man in the Moon. Ezra Jack Keats. New York: MacMillan Publishing Co., 1981. (The book tells about a boy who is unhappy because his friends laugh and call his father the "junkman". His father shows him that with great imagination using the junk they can travel through space.)

Rockets and Astronauts. Brenda Thompson and Rosemary Giesen. Minneapolis, Minnesota: Lerner Publications, 1977. (Traces the development of astronautics from the first unmanned artificial satellites through lunar landings to plans for space stations and extensive space travel.)

Rockets and Missiles. Griffith Jones. Windermere, Florida: Rourke Enterprises, Inc., 1982. (Discusses sounding rockets, orbiting, satellites used for weather, communications and mapping purposes, shuttle rocketry, and missiles. Actual photographs.)

Satellites. Kate Petty. New York: Franklin Watts, 1984. (Defines and explains satellites and their usefulness to us.)

Satellites in Outer Space. Isaac Asimov. New York: Random House, 1960. (Satellites that take pictures of the far side of the moon are described. TV programs are sent across the Atlantic by satellites as well as pictures of the real shape of the earth are shown.)

Saturn. Seymour Simon. New York: Morrow, 1985. (Saturn is described with its rings and moons. Actual photography.)

Sky Dragon. Ron Wegen. New York: Greenwillow Books, 1982. (Three children look up at snow filled clouds in the sky and see them as various animals which give them an idea of what to build out of the snow.)

The Solar System. Isaac Asimov. New York: Follett, 1975. (Introduces the solar system and the characteristics of the planets.)

Space. Rochelle Goldstein. Windermere, Florida: Rourke Enterprises, Inc., 1982. (Includes discussions of space probes, Skylab, space shuttles, solar energy, space colonies and the space telescope.)

Space. James A. Seevers. Milwaukee, Wisconsin: MacDonald-Raintree, Inc., 1978. (Defines and explains the various aspects of space exploration-gravity, rockets, satellites, manned space flights.)

Spacecraft. Michael Jay. New York: Franklin Watts, Ltd., 1980. An easy-read fact book that discusses all types of space craft and their purposes.)

Space Machines. Larry A. Ciupik and James A. Seevers. Milwaukee, Wisconsin: Raintree Children's Books, 1979. (Using photographs, describes a variety of equipment for use in space, including space laboratories and stations, mining machines and transporters.)

Space Shuttles. Margaret Friskey. Chicago: Children's Press, 1982. (Using some NASA photographs in text, the book describes the operation and use of space shuttles.)

Space Shuttle. Nigel Hawkes. New York: Gloucester Press, 1983. (Describes various space shuttles and how they work.)

Space Shuttle. Kate Petty. New York: Watts, 1984. (Describes a typical space shuttle trip including launch, flight missions, space walks, reentry and landing and looks at how shuttles may be used in the future.)

Squawk to the Moon, Little Goose. New York: Viking, 1974. (A story about a goose who learns about the moon. The theme of disobedience and self-reliance is portrayed.)

Star Boy. Paul Goble. New York: Bradbury Press, 1983. (A Blackfeet tribal tale about the sun, morning star and the people.)

Star Wars. Wayne Douglas Barlowe. New York: Random House, Inc., 1978. (A pop-up book on the characters from Star Wars. Artoo Detoo, C-3PO, Gatoonine Desert, Sandpeople riding Banthas, Chewbacca, X-wing fighter, Darth Vader, Obi-wan Kenobi, Luke; Princess and Death Star. Few words with very good illustrations and paper engineering.)

Stepping Into Space, Eyes in the Sky. David Baker. Vero Beach, Florida: Rourke Enterprises, Inc., 1986. (This book shows photographs and explains satellites, telescopes, the Skylab space station, and the Hubble space telescope.)

2-B and the Rock 'n Roll Band. Sherry Paul. Cleveland, Ohio: Modern Curriculum Press, Inc., 1981. (A picture book telling about 2-B, a robot, who no one wanted until a little boy discovered the robot's talents for singing. Thus he became useful after all.)

2-B and the Space Visitor. Sherry Paul. Cleveland, Ohio: Modern Curriculum Press, 1981. 2-B is already on earth and C-U lands on earth. Together they see all the children dressed up for Halloween. They are so scared of the earth monsters that they get back into the spaceship and go home.)

When I Go To the Moon. Claudia Lewis. New York: MacMillan Co., 1961. (This story mentions many facts about the earth as seen from the moon. A child-space explorer explains what is happening from the perspective of being on the moon.)

Why the Sky is Far Away. Mary Joan Gerson. New York: Harcourt, 1974. (The Nigerian story of the Garden of Eden.)

Why the Sun and Moon Live in the Sky. Elphinstone Dayrell. New York: Houghton Mifflin, 1968. (The African folktale of how water visited the sun and moon with so many friends that they were driven up into the sky.)

You Will Go to the Moon. Mae and Ira Freeman. New York: Random House, Inc. 1971. (A beginning reader book of a space flight to a space station and the moon.)

Additional Books

The Earth and Sky. Jeaunesse and Verdet, illus by Perols, A First Discovery Book, Scholastic, 1992.

I Want To Be An Astronaut. Byron Barton. Harper Trophy, 1992 . 32 pages (color illus.). Ages 3 to 6.

My First Book of Space. Hansen and Bell. Simon and Schuster, New York, 1985. Ages 5 to 10.

Owl Moon. Jane Yolen. Caldecott Award. Illus. by John Schoenherr. Philomel Books, New York, 1987.

Papa, Please Get the Moon for Me. Eric Carle. Picture Book Studio USA, Mass. Distributed by Alphabet Press, 1986. 25 pages. (color illus.)

Books for Teachers and Parents

All Aboard for Space. Jane Hodges, Ph.D. Education and Awareness Branch, Kennedy Space Center, FL 32899, 1992.

Journey Through Air and Space. Jane Hodges, Ph.D. 1986, revised edition 1987, ISBN 0-9618589-0-7, Library of Congress Catalog Card Number: 87-81114, Edisto Press.

The Enterprise and Beyond. Jane Hodges, Ph.D. Copyright 1988, ISBN 0-9618589-5-8, Edisto Press.

Resource Centers

Teacher Resource Centers are established to provide educators with NASA-related educational materials for use in the classroom. These materials can be referenced or duplicated at the Center to include classroom activities, lesson plans, teacher guides, laser discs, slides, audio and video tapes.

Please contact the NASA Center that serves your state for further Teacher Resource Center material or information about other available services.

NASA Ames Research Center
  Teacher Resource Center
  Mail Stop 204-7
  Moffet Field, CA 94035
  (415) 694-6077

Alaska, Arizona, California, Hawaii, Idaho, Montana, Nevada, Oregon, Utah, Washington, Wyoming

NASA Goddard Space Flight Center
  Teacher Resource Laboratory
  Mail Code 130.3
  Greenbelt, MD 20771
  (301) 286-8570

Connecticut, Delaware, District of Columbia, Maine, Maryland, Massachusetts, New Hampshire, New Jersey, New York, Pennsylvania, Rhode Island, Vermont

NASA Jet Propulsion Laboratory
  Teacher Resource Center
  Attn: JPL Education Outreach
  Mail Stop C530
  Pasadena, CA 91109
  (818) 354-6916

Serves inquiries related to space exploration and other JPL activities

NASA Lyndon B. Johnson Space Center
  Teacher Resource Room
  Code AP-4
  Houston, TX 77058
  (713) 483-8696/8618

Colorado, Kansas, Nebraska, New Mexico, North Dakota, Oklahoma, South Dakota, Texas

BIBLIOGRAPHY AND RESOURCES

NASA John F. Kennedy Space Center
  Educators Resource Laboratory
  Mail Code PA-EAB
  Kennedy Space Center, FL 32899
  (407) 867-4090/9383

Florida, Georgia, Puerto Rico, Virgin Islands

NASA Langhy Research Center
  Teacher Resource Center
  Mail Stop 146
  Hampton, VA 23665
  (804) 865-4468/3017

Kentucky, North Carolina, South Carolina, Virginia, West Virginia

NASA Lewis Research Center
  Teacher Resource Center
  Mail Stop 8-1
  Cleveland, OH 44135
  (216) 433-2017

Illinois, Indiana, Michigan, Minnesota, Ohio, Wisconsin

NASA George C. Marshall Space Flight Center
  Teacher Resource Center at
  Alabama Space and Rocket Center
  One Tranquility Base
  Huntsville, AL 35807
  (205) 544-5812

Alabama, Arkansas, Iowa, Louisiana, Mississippi, Missouri, Tennessee

NASA John C. Stennis Space Center
  Teacher Resource Center
  Building 1200
  Stennis Space Center, MS 39529
  (601) 688-3338

Mississippi

About the Author

Tonja Weimer was born in Bakersfield, California and was raised in a family of cowboys and cattle ranchers. She grew up hearing her father's auctioneering chant and the folk songs that were so much a part of the life of the Oklahomans who fled to California to escape the dust bowl. You will hear the influence of this folk heritage in her work. Starting at the age of three, Tonja was trained in ballet, tap, gymnastics, and modern dance which ultimately led to the creation of her unique movement program that is central to all of her work.

Just out of college and in her first teaching job, she sang the songs she loved to the children in her care. They kept asking for more. She discovered that her songs, rhymes, and innovative movement activities helped motivate, teach, and bring out the creativity in youngsters. As the success she had with children grew, she was asked to share her original and inspirational philosophy and techniques at conferences for educators. People kept requesting her songs and her methods for using them. So, in 1971, she started her career as a recording artist.

One of twenty National Fellows chosen by the U.S. Department of Education, she obtained an M.A in Early Childhood Education in 1968 at San Francisco State College. Tonja has been a supervisor, a director of early childhood programs, a national consultant and the owner and director of her own creative dance and music schools.

A recipient of grants from the Pittsburgh Foundation, Alcoa and the Hunt Foundations, she adapted her music and dance program to children of special needs. She was a key presenter at the 1987 Special Olympics at the request of the Kennedy Foundation.

Encouraged by NASA, she has created this book and tape to turn Space into a fun place for young children to learn science. If you are like the thousands who previewed these songs at conferences and concerts, you will love them too.

Prior to Space Songs for Children, she has produced five books, four albums, and two videos. Tonja lives in Pittsburgh with her husband, Vik Pearce, and their four children. She travels in the U.S. and abroad, speaking at conferences, doing children's concerts and making TV appearances. Her charisma makes her an artist in great demand.

OTHER MATERIALS FROM TONJA EVETTS WEIMER

These books and tapes can be obtained through your favorite book store, or ordered from PEP Publishing. P.O. Box 79117, Pittsburgh PA 15216 • Phone orders, have your VISA or Mastercard ready and call 1-800-842-9571. Shipping is 10% with a $3.00 minimum. PA residents add 6% tax. Use the order form on the last page.

Animal Friends for Sale

This release is full of favorite children's folk songs about animals. You will hear the influence of Tonja's cowboy heritage on this album and experience why children are captivated by her music. This is another album, rich in creative movement potential.

Cassette: ISBN 0-936823-06-2 $9.98

Creative Dance and Movement

A teacher's guide to Tonja's creative dance and movement program, this illustrated book includes philosophy, lesson plans and creative activity details that make it a must for the early childhood classroom.

Book $8.95

Fingerplays and Action Chants Volume One, Animals

The very best fingerplays and singing games about animals. These are instantaneous favorites and include the "Bear Hunt." Great for car trips.

Book: ISBN 0-936823-00-3 $8.95
Cassette: ISBN 0-936823-01-1 $8.95

Volume Two, Family and Friends

Tonja's favorite fingerplays and action songs about family. Children love the sound effects on the tape and stay involved for hours. Includes "My Mama Told Me," an all time favorite.

Book: ISBN 0-936823-02-X $8.95
Cassette: ISBN 0-936823-03-8 $8.95

Folk Songs for Children

An instantaneous children's favorite, especially designed for creative movement activities. Sequentially arranged folk favorites provide quiet, semi-active, then active participation, in a blend that is Tonja's specialty.

Cassette: ISBN 0-936823-05-04 $9.98

Frolicking Frogs; A Time To Sing And Dance

Folksongs, counting fingerplays and story about frogs, set the mood for children to go into the swamp and dance to "Frog Boogie".

Video: ISBN 0-936823-10-0 $19.95

Rhymes and Rainbows; A Time To Sing And Dance

Folk Songs including "Jenny Jenkins", finger plays and a story about rainbows teaches colors as the children dance with streamers under the rainbow.

Video: ISBN 0-936823-09-7 $19.95

Order Form

☎ **Telephone Orders:** Call Toll Free: 1-800-842-9571. Have your Visa or Master Card ready.

✳ **FAX Orders** (412) 571-1217

✉ **Postal Order:** PEP Publishing, P.O. Box 79117, Pittsburgh, PA 15216, USA. (412) 344-5451

Please send the following. I understand that I may return anything for a full refund–for any reason, no questions asked.

Item	Price
_____	_____
_____	_____
_____	_____
_____	_____
_____	_____

Subtotal _____

PA residents
Add 6 % Tax _____

Shipping: Book Rate: 10% with $3.00 minimum.
(Surface shipping may take three to four weeks)
Air Mail: $4.00 per item.

Shipping _____

Total _____

❏ Please send me Tonja's brochure FREE.

Company Name: _____

Name: _____

Address: _____

City: _____ State: _____ Zip: _____

Telephone _____

Payments: ❏ Check   ❏ Credit Card: ❏ Visa   ❏ Mastercard

Card Number _____

Name on Card _____ Exp. Date _____